A Roman Journey

Alex Woolf

HODDER
Wayland

an imprint of Hodder Children's Books

Produced for Hodder Wayland by
Discovery Books Ltd
Unit 3, 37 Watling Street, Leintwardine, Shropshire SY7 0LW, England

First published in 2003 by Hodder Wayland, an imprint of
Hodder Children's Books

British Library Cataloguing in Publication Data
Woolf, Alex
A Roman journey. - (History journeys)
1. Transportation - Great Britain - History - To 1500 - Juvenile literature 2. Great
Britain - History - Roman period, 55B.C. -449 A.D. - Juvenile literature
I. Title
388' .09361'09015

0 7502 3959 X

Printed and bound by G. Canale & C. S.p.A. Italy

Designer: Ian Winton
Editor: Rebecca Hunter
Illustrator: Mark Bergin

Hodder Children's Books would like to thank the following
for the loan of their material:

Ancient Art and Architecture: pages 9, 10 (top), 19 (middle), 27;
British Museum: pages 4, 5 (both); **Colchester Museum**: page 13 (bottom);
Corbis: *cover*, **Discovery Picture Library**: pages 12, 14, 15, 18, 19 (bottom), 21
(both), 25 (bottom); **Fortean Picture Library**: pages 23 & 25 (Janet & Colin Bord);
Museum of London: pages 10 (bottom), 11 (Peter Froste); **Photo AKG London**:
pages 6 (Peter Connolly), 7 (top Erich Lessing), 7 (bottom), 9, 16 (Erich Lessing),
17 (top Gilles Mermet), 17 (bottom Erich Lessing), 19 (top) & 20 (Erich Lessing),
24 & 26 (Peter Connolly), 27 & 29 (both) (Erich Lessing),
28 (Gilles Mermet); **Rebecca Hunter**: page 13 (top).

Hodder Children's Books
A division of Hodder Headline Limited
338 Euston Road
London NW1 3BH

CONTENTS

ROMANS IN BRITAIN

It is the year AD 208. Julius Gallicus is a Roman legionary who was born in Gaul (present-day France). He has been recruited by the Emperor Septimius Severus as part of the force to help stamp out an uprising by the Caledonian tribe in Britain at the northern border of the Roman Empire.

A Roman bust of the emperor Claudius. During his visit to Britain, Claudius accepted the surrender of eleven of the British tribal leaders.

Britain had been part of the Roman Empire for 165 years by the time of Julius Gallicus' arrival there. The invasion of Britain had taken place in AD 43. Claudius, the emperor at that time, sent a force numbering about 40,000 men under the command of Aulus Plautius.

BOUDICCA'S REBELLION

Boudicca was a queen of the Iceni tribe who led a rebellion in AD 60-1. After the Romans stole Iceni land and assaulted her and her daughters, she gathered a force of many thousands, and attacked and burned the Roman towns of Camulodunum (Colchester), Londinium (London) and Verulamium (St Albans). Her army was finally defeated by a Roman force under Suetonius Paulinus. Rather than being taken alive, Boudicca poisoned herself.

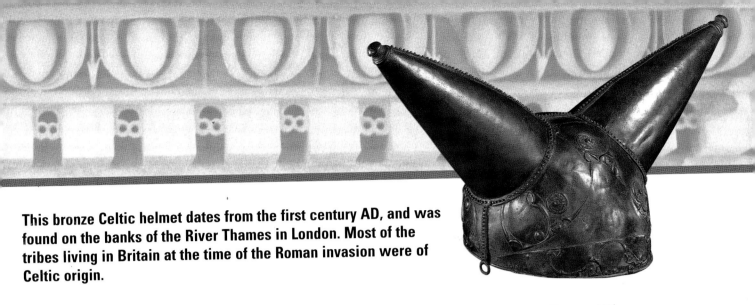

This bronze Celtic helmet dates from the first century AD, and was found on the banks of the River Thames in London. Most of the tribes living in Britain at the time of the Roman invasion were of Celtic origin.

At that time Britain was made up of many different tribes. There was no united response to the invasion, and the hastily gathered British army was no match for the highly trained legionaries. When news of the first victories reached Rome, Claudius himself came to Britain to witness the taking of Camulodunum (Colchester), which he declared should be the capital of the new Roman province. Within four years the invaders had conquered all of southern England and were making deep inroads into the north and west.

Britain remained part of the Roman Empire for the next 364 years. The Romans secured their conquest by building many towns and forts. These were connected by a network of roads to allow swift movement of troops and supplies. The towns were administered by tribal chieftains who had sworn loyalty to the emperor.

The Romans faced stern resistance to their rule in Scotland and eventually abandoned their plan of conquering the whole island. The emperor Hadrian ordered a wall to be built which marked the northern boundary of the empire.

The Celts protected themselves in battle with huge bronze shields almost the height of a man. These were often decorated with swirling patterns.

ROMAN SOLDIERS

Julius is 22 years old. He volunteered to join the army four years ago and he has yet to experience battle. He left his family in Lugdunum (Lyon) in present-day France knowing he might never see them again. Nevertheless he was excited at the thought of seeing the world, and attracted by the offer of a secure, well-paid profession.

A modern painting of a Roman legion on parade during the late first century AD. The ten cohorts are distinguished here by colour, each grouped into centuries. The legion also contains 120 horsemen.

Between 40,000 and 55,000 soldiers were stationed in Britain during the Roman occupation. They came from many different parts of the Empire, and by the time of Julius' arrival, many soldiers were being recruited from the local population in Britain.

The Roman army was organized into divisions of between 3,000 and 6,000 soldiers, called legions. The vast majority were foot soldiers, of which there were ten cohorts in each legion. The cohorts were further divided into centuries, each of 80 men, and these were led by centurions. Most recruits to the legions were between 18 and 22 years of age.

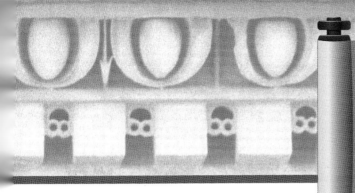

Words carved on a gravestone at South Shields tell of the love of a Syrian-born soldier for his British wife: 'To the spirits of the departed and to Regina, his freedwoman and wife, a Catuvellaunian by tribe, aged thirty; Barates of Palmyra set this up.' Next to this Latin text, Barates added in his native script: 'Regina, the freedwoman of Barates, alas.'

They would sign up for twenty-five years of service. By the second century AD, rebellions were rare in Roman Britain, and most soldiers would have spent little time actually fighting. They would be kept occupied with drills, training, route marches, and fort-building exercises.

This stone relief shows two Roman legionaries. One carries a gladius, or short sword, and shield, while the other carries a pilum, or spear.

The Roman army was highly disciplined, and punishments were severe. Theft or desertion were punishable by being beaten to death by comrades. Cowardice in battle could lead to decimation, which meant the execution of every tenth man in the guilty unit. The survivors were put on a ration of barley. Those soldiers who lived to retirement would receive some land and a regular income. Many soldiers in Britain remained in the province that had been their home for 25 years, and married local women.

This bronze Roman helmet dates from the early second century AD, and was discovered in Jerusalem in Israel. It is an 'Imperial Gallic' style of helmet, which had a large neck guard at the back.

7

CROSSING THE SEA

Julius and his fellow legionaries board the troop ship at the port of Gesoriacum (Boulogne). It is a slender, oak-built rowing ship with a team of twenty oarsmen. This is Julius' first time at sea. The crossing is rough, and he feels sick. He prays to Mercury, the god of travellers, that they will be delivered safely to Britain.

The main function of the Roman classis or fleet was to support the operations of the army. The Channel and the North Sea, with their strong tides and frequent storms, made life very difficult for Roman sailors, more used to navigating the almost tideless Mediterranean.

Some of the towns and roads in Roman Britain. Julius' journey is marked.

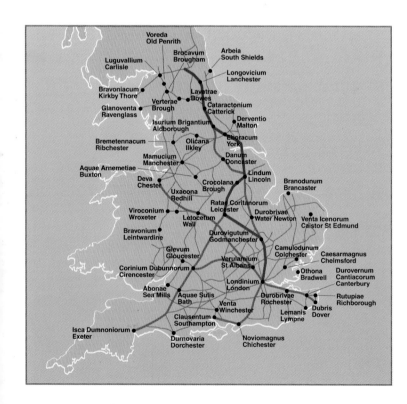

Voreda
Old Penrith
Luguvallium
Carlisle
Brocavum
Brougham
Arbeia
South Shields
Longovicium
Lanchester
Bravoniacum
Kirkby Thore
Lavatrae
Bowes
Verterae
Brough
Cataractonium
Catterick
Glanoventa
Ravenglass
Isurium Brigantium
Aldborough
Derventio
Malton
Bremetennacum
Ribchester
Olicana
Ilkley
Eboracum
York
Mamucium
Manchester
Danum
Doncaster
Aquae Arnemetiae
Buxton
Deva
Chester
Crocolana
Brough
Lindum
Lincoln
Branodunum
Brancaster
Uxacona
Redhill
Ratae Coritanorum
Leicester
Viroconium
Wroxeter
Letocetum
Wall
Durobrivae
Water Newton
Venta Icenorum
Caistor St Edmund
Bravonium
Leintwardine
Durovigutum
Godmanchester
Glevum
Gloucester
Verulamium
St Albans
Camulodunum
Colchester
Caesarmagnus
Chelmsford
Corinium Dubunnorum
Cirencester
Londinium
London
Othona
Bradwell
Durovernum
Cantiacorum
Canterbury
Abonae
Sea Mills
Aquae Sulis
Bath
Venta
Winchester
Durobrivae
Rochester
Rutupiae
Richborough
Isca Dumnoniorum
Exeter
Clausentum
Southampton
Lemanis
Lympne
Dubris
Dover
Durnovaria
Dorchester
Noviomagnus
Chichester

Nevertheless, the Roman fleet played an important part in the conquest and occupation of Britain by keeping the army well-supplied with equipment and reinforcements. In AD 83 the fleet helped in the attempted conquest of Scotland by making raids on the Scottish east coast. Some of these ships actually managed to circumnavigate Scotland, reaching the Orkney Islands, and proving that Britain was an island.

THE QUINQUEREME

The most successful warship of Roman times was a long slender ship called the quinquereme. It had three levels of oars, the top two being worked by two men, and the bottom by one. A common method of attack was to ram opposing ships with its heavy bronze beak fitted below the waterline, which could punch a hole in an enemy ship's hull.

This relief containing Roman galleys is part of Trajan's Column in Rome, which dates from the first century AD. The design of Roman warships was greatly influenced by the Greeks and the Phoenicians.

Most seaborne traffic, however, went to the port of London. In Roman times the Thames was beyond the reach of the tides, making it very easy to navigate. As well as London, Roman ports were also built at Dover and Richborough for ships crossing to or from Boulogne. There were also harbours at the Tyne, the Wash, Southampton and Exeter.

The Roman navy used oared warships and transport vessels, and sailing ships. Each ship was commanded by a trierarch and a centurion, and was manned by a small force of infantry, as well as rowers.

ARRIVING IN LONDINIUM

Julius is impressed by the port of Londinium, with over half a mile of waterfront crowded with barges and ships, their cargoes being unloaded. The quayside is thronged with soldiers, sailors and merchants. The legionaries disembark. They march to the fort where they will be lodging for the night. Outside they see slaves at work building the city wall.

(*Below*) Here is a model of a London waterfront scene in about AD 100. A cargo of amphorae (clay jars) is being unloaded from a ship, to be stored in one of the warehouses that line the quay.

The city of London was a Roman creation. There was a small Celtic settlement there before they arrived, but it was the Romans who saw the benefits of locating a city at the first point where the Thames could be bridged.

The new city grew quickly and was already a centre of trade when it was burned to the ground by Boudicca's army in AD 60. London was soon rebuilt, and replaced Colchester as the capital of the province. By the end of the first century AD, London had become established as Britain's commercial and political centre.

This modern painting shows an aerial view of how Londinium might have looked around AD 250. The town hall and market square are clearly visible in the centre of the city, and the army fort can be seen in the northwest, near the amphitheatre.

Fine public buildings were constructed to suit its status as an important Roman city, including temples, public baths and government buildings. The governor's palace was built beside the Thames, with large halls and a 35-metre garden pond with a fountain. The largest building in the city was the town hall. Next to it lay an impressive 3 hectare market square.

- 'London' is a Celtic word - perhaps deriving from the name of a farm or tribal chief from that area.

- The population of Roman London was between 12,000 and 20,000.

- In Roman times, the Thames was 300 metres wide (today it is 100 metres wide).

The fort where Julius and his fellow legionaries lodged was built around AD 120. It was situated on the northwest edge of the city, and housed the governor's guard. It was 200 metres square with rounded corner towers and a gate in each side. When Julius arrived in AD 208, a six-metre-high defensive wall was being constructed around the city, which included part of the wall around the fort.

A VISIT TO THE AMPHITHEATRE

The legionaries are off-duty for the remainder of the day. Julius and a few others decide to go and watch the games at the nearby amphitheatre. The climax of the show is a combat to the death between two helmeted gladiators. They are Samnites, who fight with oblong shields and short swords. Julius is pleased because his favourite wins.

The Roman theatre in Verulamium was built around AD 130, and was rediscovered in 1847. It is one of the few Roman theatres found in Britain.

Theatres and amphitheatres were built all over the Roman Empire, and remains have been found in Britain in places like Dorchester, Chichester and St Albans, as well as London. The amphitheatre in Londinium was initially a wooden structure, built in AD 70 at the northwest edge of the city just south of the fort. In AD 170 it was rebuilt in stone.

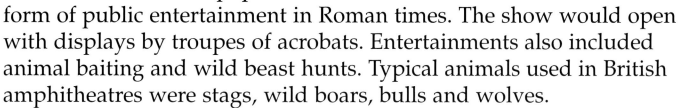

This fragment from a Roman relief shows another popular entertainment: gladiators were sometimes sent into the arena to fight wild animals such as lions and bears.

The games performed in these arenas were the most popular form of public entertainment in Roman times. The show would open with displays by troupes of acrobats. Entertainments also included animal baiting and wild beast hunts. Typical animals used in British amphitheatres were stags, wild boars, bulls and wolves.

The climax of the show was always a fight to the death between two gladiators. 'Gladiator' means 'swordsman', from the Latin gladius, 'sword'. They were usually slaves, prisoners of war, or criminals. Occasionally, female gladiators fought in the arena. There were various classes of gladiator: as well as Samnites there were Thraces who were armed with a small round shield and a curved dagger; they were generally pitted against mirmillones who had a helmet, sword and shield.

If a gladiator found himself at the mercy of his opponent, he lifted his finger to beg for salvation from the crowd. If the spectators wished him spared, they waved their handkerchiefs. But if they desired him to be killed they turned their thumbs downward.

A gladiatorial contest is shown on this Roman pottery vase found in Colchester. Here a defeated *retiarius* (right), in combat with a secutor, raises his finger for mercy.

ROMAN ROADS

The legionaries leave early the next day, taking the major road to the northeast, Ermine Street. They march in full uniform, carrying their weapons and other kit. Their pace is swift on the ruler-straight gravel road. The landscape is stark and threatening, covered in thorny bushes or thick forest. Julius measures their progress by counting off the roadside milestones.

The Romans were remarkable road-builders. Archaeologists have traced more than 9,600 km of major Roman roads in Britain, as well as many more miles of minor roads and paths.

The roads were originally built to carry the soldiers and military supplies that enabled the conquest of Britain. They gradually came to be shared by other traffic – merchants, traders, couriers and government officials. Roads were the lifelines that kept remote garrisons supplied with food and materials, and allowed messages to be swiftly sent. A body of soldiers could cover up to 48 kilometres a day on these roads, carrying kit weighing 23 kilograms.

Blackstone Edge Roman road runs over the Pennines between Rochdale and Elland in South Yorkshire. Paved Roman roads like this one were quite unusual; most were surfaced with gravel or small stones.

14

Roman road-building techniques were similar throughout the Empire. An agger, or embankment, was built using the earth and stones dug up from either side, leaving ditches for drainage. Chalk or limestone provided a solid base on which gravel, broken flints or smaller stones were laid. When first built, Roman roads in Britain were about six metres wide. By AD 120 the width of most main roads averaged thirteen metres.

The Romans built their roads extremely straight. One stretch of the Roman-built Fosse Way never deviates more than 9.5 km from a straight line over its 320-km length. Military engineers achieved this by standing on high ground, and plotting each length of road in turn.

Repair and resurfacing of the roads was the responsibility of the civitates, or local authorities, based in the major towns of the province. They were also responsible for setting up milestones along the main roads, so that travellers could see the distance to the nearest town. Almost a hundred of these survive with their carved inscriptions still readable.

A Roman milestone at Chesterholm in Northumberland. Milestones were erected at every Roman mile (1,480m) along major roads. They were usually cylindrical in shape, up to 1.8 metres high and 45 cm in diameter. Inscribed on them was a mileage figure and the name of the town from which it was measured.

STAYING AT AN INN
– Durovigutum

Rich or high-ranking Romans had their own personal cupbearers who would serve them with drinks. This fragment of a Roman relief shows a cupbearer at a bar carrying a drinking-vessel.

After two days, the legionaries reach Durovigutum (Godmanchester) which has a large mansio or inn. Here the weary soldiers wash off the sweat of the day's march in the bath-house before enjoying a good dinner. Most of the legionaries pass the final part of the evening in the tavern, but Julius prefers to go for a quiet stroll around the garden.

As the traffic increased on Roman roads, so mansiones were established to cater for travellers. They were spaced at 30- to 50-kilometre intervals, and provided meeting places for merchants and traders, rooms and refreshment for foot soldiers, and stables for messengers on horseback.

All mansiones followed a similar design, with the accommodation grouped around a central courtyard or garden. Many had separate bath-houses and exercise halls.

THE IMPERIAL MESSENGER SERVICE

In the first century BC, the Romans established the *Cursus Publicus*, or imperial communications service. A network of post-houses and mansiones were set up along the major roads throughout the Empire, including Britain. Couriers could get fresh horses at post-houses, set 15 to 25 kilometres apart, enabling them to cover about 80 kilometres a day.

This Tunisian mosaic shows dice players in a tavern. Gambling was a common activity in the taverns of Roman inns. A pair of dice were shaken in a cup and tossed. Bets were placed on the number they showed.

The mansio at Godmanchester was, by AD 208, one of the largest and finest in the country. The reception and dining rooms both had mosaic floors and plastered, painted walls. The bedrooms were arranged in two rows down the long sides of the building, and there may have been an upper floor of bedrooms as well.

There was a bath-house to the rear of the inn with separate changing rooms for men and women. Guests at the mansio could also make use of a number of shops and smithies (for horseshoes), and a small temple dedicated to the native god Abandinus.

These dice, which the Romans called tesserae, were made out of bone.

Sometimes mansiones led to the development of towns. The siting of a mansio at Chelmsford in the late first century AD was followed by the building of some shops, including a bakery, a dye-works, and some taverns. Before long, a small town had appeared.

THE BATH-HOUSE –
Ratae Coritanorum

The Great Bath of Aquae Sulis (now Bath in Avon). This lay at the centre of an elaborate complex of five baths, built by the Romans above natural hot springs. Aquae Sulis also contained a great temple dedicated to the Celtic goddess, Sulis.

Two days later, the soldiers arrive at Ratae Coritanorum (Leicester), well-known for its fine public baths. The soldiers are keen to try them. Their shouts and splashes echo noisily around the stone chambers. Julius finishes with a massage and a dip in the cold plunge. Afterwards, he and his friends play a game of dice in the exercise yard.

The public bath was a very important part of Roman social life. It was the place for business deals, gambling, exercise and gossip. Visitors left their clothes in niches or cupboards in the undressing room, or they paid someone to look after them. From here they entered the frigidarium (cold room) where bathers could sprinkle themselves with water from a basin, or the bolder ones could jump into a large cold bath.

The Roman philosopher, Seneca, who lived above a public baths in the first century AD, was disturbed by 'shouts, grunts, slaps – and the screams of those who were having their armpits plucked.'

18

A bather's strigil. Once he had begun to sweat, the bather would pour olive oil on his body. Then the oil, along with any sweat and dirt on the skin, was scraped off with the curved metal blade of the strigil.

A first century AD case containing make-up tools. Roman baths contained women's dressing rooms, where women could spend time applying cosmetics and grooming themselves.

Bathers then moved into the tepidarium (warm room) where they oiled their bodies and felt the steam open their pores. They then had a choice of hot rooms – the caldarium with its dense steam, or the laconium, a dry-heat chamber. After a hot-water bath, the bathers reversed the route, ending with a dip in the cold pool to close the pores. The discovery of tweezers, earpicks and nail-cleaners at some bath-houses suggests that people could obtain other treatments too.

The baths were open all day. Women used them in the morning, and men in the afternoon and evening. They were heated by an under-floor central-heating system called a hypocaust. The public baths in towns like Leicester, Chichester and Wroxeter may have been used by up to 500 people a day.

This is the furnace used for heating the water at the large public bath-house at the Roman town of Viroconium (now Wroxeter in Shropshire).

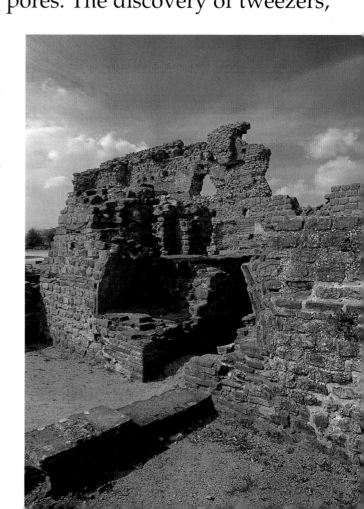

GODS AND GODDESSES

As the legionaries progress northwards, the locals seem more hostile. Sometimes they spit at the soldiers. Julius is nearly hit by a stone. At Eboracum, Julius' fears are eased by the sight of the many statues to Roman gods and goddesses. At the temple of Mars he prays for the war god's help in the coming battles against the barbarians.

Jupiter, depicted in this second century AD statue, was the king of the Roman gods. Originally the god of the sky, Jupiter was worshipped as god of rain, thunder and lightning.

The Romans worshipped many different gods, each of which was associated with a different activity. The most important gods were Jupiter, Juno and Minerva. Jupiter was the most powerful god, who could be called upon to protect both the individual and the state. Juno was the goddess of women and childbirth, and Minerva the goddess of healing. Beneath them were gods such as Mercury who protected travellers and merchants, Apollo the god of music and healing, and Venus the goddess of love.

The Romans were usually tolerant of the religious beliefs of conquered peoples. They accepted and even worshipped some of the local Celtic gods, seeing similarities between them and their own gods. For example, the Romans associated the Celtic god Sulis with Minerva. Throughout Britain, temples and shrines were built to Celtic gods and their Roman equivalents.

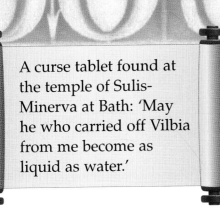

A curse tablet found at the temple of Sulis-Minerva at Bath: 'May he who carried off Vilbia from me become as liquid as water.'

Remains of a third century AD temple to Mithras at Carrawburgh on Hadrian's Wall. The worshippers of Mithras were divided into seven grades. To enter a new grade involved passing severe tests such as ordeals of heat, cold and fasting. An 'ordeal pit' has been found at Carrawburgh close to a large fire.

The temple priests wore robes and bronze or silver jewelled headbands. Worshippers brought offerings such as small figurines, jewellery, or a live sheep, which they laid before the altar. Some brought curse tablets, rolled-up sheets of lead on which they had scratched a plea to the god to punish a person who had wronged them.

A religious cult that gained particular popularity with the Roman army throughout the Empire during the second and third century AD was Mithraism. Mithras was the Persian god of light and truth. He encouraged physical and moral strength in his followers, increasing his appeal to soldiers. Five Mithraic temples have been found in Britain, including a famous one in London.

Three altars found at the temple at Carrawburgh. Each of these contain dedications to Mithras from soldiers who served at the fort.

REACHING HADRIAN'S WALL

The legionaries finally reach their destination: Hadrian's Wall – the edge of the Roman Empire. They have been travelling for twelve days, covering 463 kilometres. Julius climbs some steps to the top of the Wall. It winds over hills and valleys, disappearing over the horizon in either direction. He looks out across the barren empty lands beyond. There is no sign of the Caledonians.

Today, Hadrian's Wall is officially recognized as a World Heritage Site. The best-preserved sections of the Wall are about one metre high.

Hadrian's Wall was built on the orders of the emperor Hadrian following his visit to Britain in AD 122. He saw the need for a physical border between Roman Britain and the independent tribes to the north, to control the movement of people and goods, and to help defend the province from attack.

However, the Wall's main purpose was political, not military. It marked the northern limits of the Roman Empire, and was intended as a permanent line separating the barbarians to the north from the civilized world of the Romans.

- Hadrian's Wall was the largest structure ever built by the Romans.
- About two million tonnes of stone were used in the construction of Hadrian's Wall.
- Almost 2,000 wooden writing tablets were found at Vindolanda, one of the 17 large forts on Hadrian's Wall.
- Hadrian's Wall was breached three times in its history: in AD 197, 296 and 367.

The Wall runs from coast to coast for 113 kilometres between Carlisle in the west and South Shields in the east. It took 14 years to build and by AD 136 it was complete. However, it continued to be modified and improved over the years. In its final form it was a stone wall 4.25 to 4.65 metres high and 2.4 to 3 metres thick. On its north side was a ditch to make it more difficult to attack. To the south of the Wall was the Vallum, a flat-bottomed ditch with earthen mounds to either side. This was built to prevent civilians from gaining access to the Wall. Soldiers could reach the Wall via guarded causeways across the Vallum.

The Wall fell into neglect and disrepair during certain periods of the Roman occupation. When the Romans left Britain in AD 407, Hadrian's Wall no longer had a purpose. In the years that followed, many of its stones were taken away and used in the construction of local buildings.

The north gate of Vercovicium Roman Fort on Hadrian's Wall. The fort was one of twelve situated along the Wall. Vercovicium means 'the Place of Fighters'.

MANNING THE FORT

Julius is separated from his travelling companions, and sent to Vercovicium, one of the forts on the Wall. The following morning he reports to the praetorium, the largest building in the fort, where the commander lives with his family. After receiving a personal greeting from the commander, Julius joins the other legionaries and auxiliary soldiers of the fort in the assembly hall, where the orders of the day are read out.

A reconstruction of Vercovicium Fort showing how it might have looked in the third century AD. The vicus (civilian settlement) can be seen to the right of the fort, with the principias (headquarters) and praetorium (commander's house) in the centre.

All the way along Hadrian's Wall, small forts, called milecastles, were built at intervals of a Roman mile (1,480 metres). Each milecastle could house units of up to thirty men. There were seventeen milecastles in all, each containing between five hundred and a thousand troops. Between each milecastle were two evenly spaced towers where sentries kept watch. The plan was that every part of the Wall would be visible during daylight.

Larger forts were built at strategic points, which had barracks to accommodate up to 1,000 troops each. When the Wall was threatened, troops would pour out of the north gates of the forts and milecastles to confront the attackers.

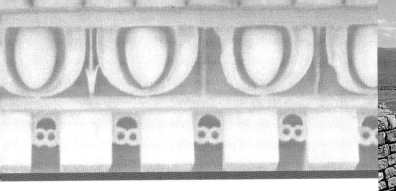

The granaries at Vercovicium had vents in the outer walls and floors raised on stone pillars, to allow air to circulate. It was originally a single building, but was split into two in the third century AD.

Vercovicium contained thirteen barrack blocks, where the soldiers lived and slept. Each block was capable of holding a century (80 men). Food was stored in granaries, which had floors suspended on stone pillars to keep the food cool and dry and free of vermin.

Most forts had wells. However, Vercovicium obtained its water supply by collecting rainwater in tanks via a system of channels and drains. These tanks were also used to flush out the lavatories.

The lavatories at Vercovicium. Wooden seats would have been fitted in a row on each side directly over the main sewer. The two water channels in the centre would have been used by soldiers to wash the sponges that served the purpose of toilet paper.

HOSPITALS

Soldiers in the Roman army were more likely to die from disease than from battle wounds. The Romans were well aware of this risk and troops based at Hadrian's Wall were provided with a good standard of medical care. The hospital at Vercovicium contained a surgery, small rooms for staff and patients, and a courtyard for growing medicinal herbs.

MARCHING INTO BATTLE

The soldiers are patrolling the Wall north of Vercovicium. The Caledonians emerge waving spears and charging. Julius is scared, but remembers his training. The legionaries let fly with their javelins, striking the shields of the attackers. Before the enemy can recover, the Romans are upon them, forcing them back with their iron shield bosses and stabbing them with their short swords.

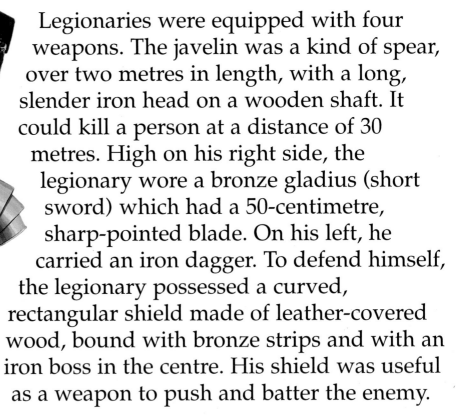

Legionaries were equipped with four weapons. The javelin was a kind of spear, over two metres in length, with a long, slender iron head on a wooden shaft. It could kill a person at a distance of 30 metres. High on his right side, the legionary wore a bronze gladius (short sword) which had a 50-centimetre, sharp-pointed blade. On his left, he carried an iron dagger. To defend himself, the legionary possessed a curved, rectangular shield made of leather-covered wood, bound with bronze strips and with an iron boss in the centre. His shield was useful as a weapon to push and batter the enemy.

Pieces of Roman armour found at the Roman fort at Corbridge, Northumberland. These form parts of a soldier's cuirass, or body armour, such as shoulder plates (1), breast plates (2) and girth hoops (3). In the centre are reconstructions of the pieces of a cuirass.

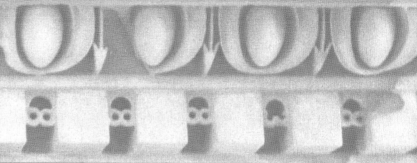

A stone relief from the early second century AD showing a barbarian fighting a Roman legionary. When fighting the Celts, Roman tactics involved getting in very close to the enemy for hand-to-hand fighting. The gladius proved more useful in these situations than the long Celtic sword.

In battle, the legionaries usually stood in the centre and provided the main thrust of the attack, with the cavalry positioned at the sides. Auxiliary units (support troops) fought on the wings or were held in reserve. Legionaries were trained to fight in a strict pattern of disciplined formations.

To overcome Celtic strongholds such as Maiden Castle or Hod Hill, the Romans used ballistas (missile launchers) to provide a continuous barrage of iron bolts. The attack might then be led by a testudo, or 'tortoise', a formation of 27 men arranged in four ranks who locked their shields overhead and on all sides to give all round protection.

BALLISTAS

These siege weapons resembled sophisticated crossbows, and were used against British hill-forts. They fired iron bolts, or sometimes stone balls, with great accuracy, and could kill at up to 365 metres. About fifty ballistas would be used during a siege.

MEALS AND LETTER HOME

Exhausted after the fight, Julius returns to the fort at Vercovicium, grateful to have survived his first battle. He shares a meal of bread, vegetable soup, mutton and wine with his comrades. Before going to sleep, Julius writes a letter to his parents back in Lugdunum, telling them of all his experiences.

A letter found at Chesterholm contained the following: 'I have sent you ..... pairs of socks from Sattua, two pairs of sandals and two pairs of underpants...'

(TAB. VINDOL. II.346)

A legionary paid for his food himself, costing him about a third of his year's wages. His basic ration consisted of wheat – which he could grind into flour – soup, vegetables, lard (pork fat), and meat. The usual drink was sour wine or vinegar. The choice of vegetables included beans, cabbage, celery and lentils, and the meat might be pork, beef, lamb, veal or goat.

Records found at Chesterholm and Vindolanda, show that supplies of exotic foods such as venison, spices and garlic were sometimes received for the garrison commander rather than the troops. However, occasional treats such as plums, olives and Spanish wine managed to find their way into the milecastles and watchtowers on Hadrian's Wall, judging from inscriptions on amphorae (clay jars) found there.

A third century Roman mosaic from Tunisia showing the ingredients of a banquet: baskets of fruit and vegetables surrounding a gazelle. Rich Romans enjoyed dining on unusual or exotic foods, such as sow's udder, flamingo, and molluscs 'harvested under a waxing moon'.

A second or third century stone relief of Romans eating dinner. Cena (dinner) was the main meal of the day, and consisted of at least three courses.

Like many forts on the Wall, Vercovicium had a small civilian settlement, or vicus, attached to it with taverns and shops. The soldiers could go there in their off-duty hours and purchase food to supplement their rations.

Tablets at Vindolanda reveal the prices soldiers had to pay for certain goods. For example, a towel cost 2 denarii and a cloak cost 5 denarii (legionaries earned about 300 denarii a year). To avoid these extra expenses, some soldiers wrote letters to their families asking for money or clothing or for a kind of food they missed.

The Roman army in Britain was gradually weakened from the middle of the third century AD. Troops were withdrawn to fight on other frontiers of the Empire. Meanwhile, Britain's coasts were increasingly threatened by Scots, Picts, Saxons and Franks. The rich moved to the comparative safety of towns, and villas were abandoned. The last soldiers of the Roman army finally left Britain in AD 407.

A stone relief showing a scene in a Roman bakery. Bread was the basis of the Roman soldier's diet.

TIMELINE

55/54 BC — Julius Caesar invades, but does not conquer Britain.

Late 1st century BC — *Cursus Publicus* – the Roman postal service established.

AD 43 — Romans under Claudius invade Britain and establish first Roman-British city at Colchester. Eleven British kings surrender to Claudius.

c. AD 43-45 — Watling Street is built.

c. AD 45-47 — Fosse Way is built.

c. AD 50s — Ermine Street is built.

AD 60/61 — Boudicca leads a rebellion against the Romans.

AD 75-77 — The conquest of Britain is completed.

AD 79 — Agricola, the provincial governor, invades Scotland.

AD 75-100 — London transformed into a Roman city.

Early 2nd century AD — London recognized as the provincial capital.

c. AD 120 — Godmanchester mansio and bath-house built.

c. AD 122 — Hadrian approved building of a chain of canals as supply routes between the Fens and York.

AD 122-136 — Hadrian's Wall is built.

c. AD 150 — Baths at Leicester built.

Late 2nd century AD — Development of York. Many public buildings and monuments erected, including Temple of Mars.

AD 197 — Caledonians break through the Wall and devastate northern England.

AD 208 — The emperor Septimius Severus comes to Britain with a large army to deal with the Caledonian uprising, and repair damage to the Wall.
London city wall is built.

AD 209 — Caledonians surrender.

c. AD 240 — Temple of Mithras is built in London.

AD 350-400 — The Romans begin to leave Britain, as they struggle to defend their Empire closer to Rome.

AD 407 — The last Romans leave Britain.

GLOSSARY

amphitheatre — An oval arena surrounded by rising tiers of seats. These were used for many forms of entertainment.

amphora — A jar, usually made of clay, with a narrow neck and two handles, used by the ancient Greeks and Romans for holding oil, wine or certain foods.

auxiliary units — The second line of the Roman army, made up of soldiers who were not Roman citizens. They signed on for twenty-five years, and their reward on retirement was a grant of citizenship.

boss — A round raised area that sticks out of a surface, for example a stud at the centre of a shield.

Caledonians — Inhabitants of the northern part of Scotland during the Roman occupation of Britain. They were described by the Roman historian Tacitus as being 'red-haired and large of limb'.

Catuvellaunian — A member of the Catuvellauni - a tribe descended from the Belgae of northern France, and inhabiting the area of present-day Hertfordshire. The Catuvellauni were the dominant tribe in the southeast of Britain at the time of the Roman invasion.

causeway — A raised path over a ditch or area of water.

cavalry — The part of an army made up of soldiers trained to fight on horseback.

centurion — In ancient Rome, an officer in charge of a unit of 80 foot soldiers.

circumnavigate — Sail around something, such as an island.

civitates — A town council.

cohort — An ancient Roman military unit that formed one tenth of a legion and consisted of 300 to 600 men.

denarii — Plural of 'denarius' - an ancient Roman silver coin originally worth ten asses. A gold denarius was worth 25 silver denarii.

figurine — A small ornamental figure, often pottery or metal.

Fosse Way — A major Roman road which runs diagonally across Britain from Topsham in Devon to Leicester and Lincoln, probably built to serve a line of frontier forts in the early years of the conquest.

garrison — A body of troops stationed at a military post, or a military post where troops are stationed.

hypocaust — A furnace, fired by charcoal, wood or coal, that pumped hot air through channels beneath the floor of a room. Both heat and gases escaped through flues behind the walls, creating an early central-heating system.

legionary — A member of a Roman legion.

post-houses — Places established on the major roads of the Roman Empire where messengers of the imperial communications service could get a change of horse.

quayside — A platform that runs along the edge of a port or harbour, where boats are loaded and unloaded.

shrine — A place of worship.

smithies — Plural of 'smithy' - the place where a blacksmith works.

theatre — Theatres had a stage at one end surrounded by seats. They were used for plays and singing entertainments.

trierarch — A ship's captain in the Roman navy. He shared command of his vessel with a centurion, who was in charge of military aspects.

venison — The meat of a deer.

FURTHER READING

What Happened Here? Roman Palace, Tim Wood, A&C Black, 2000.

A Day in the Life of a Roman Centurion, Richard Wood, Hodder Wayland, 2000.

Pinpoints: Roman Fort, Stephen Johnson, Hodder Wayland, 2000.

You Wouldn't Want to be a Roman Gladiator, John Malam, Hodder Wayland, 2001.

INDEX